Backyard Wonders
What's Hiding in Your Backyard?

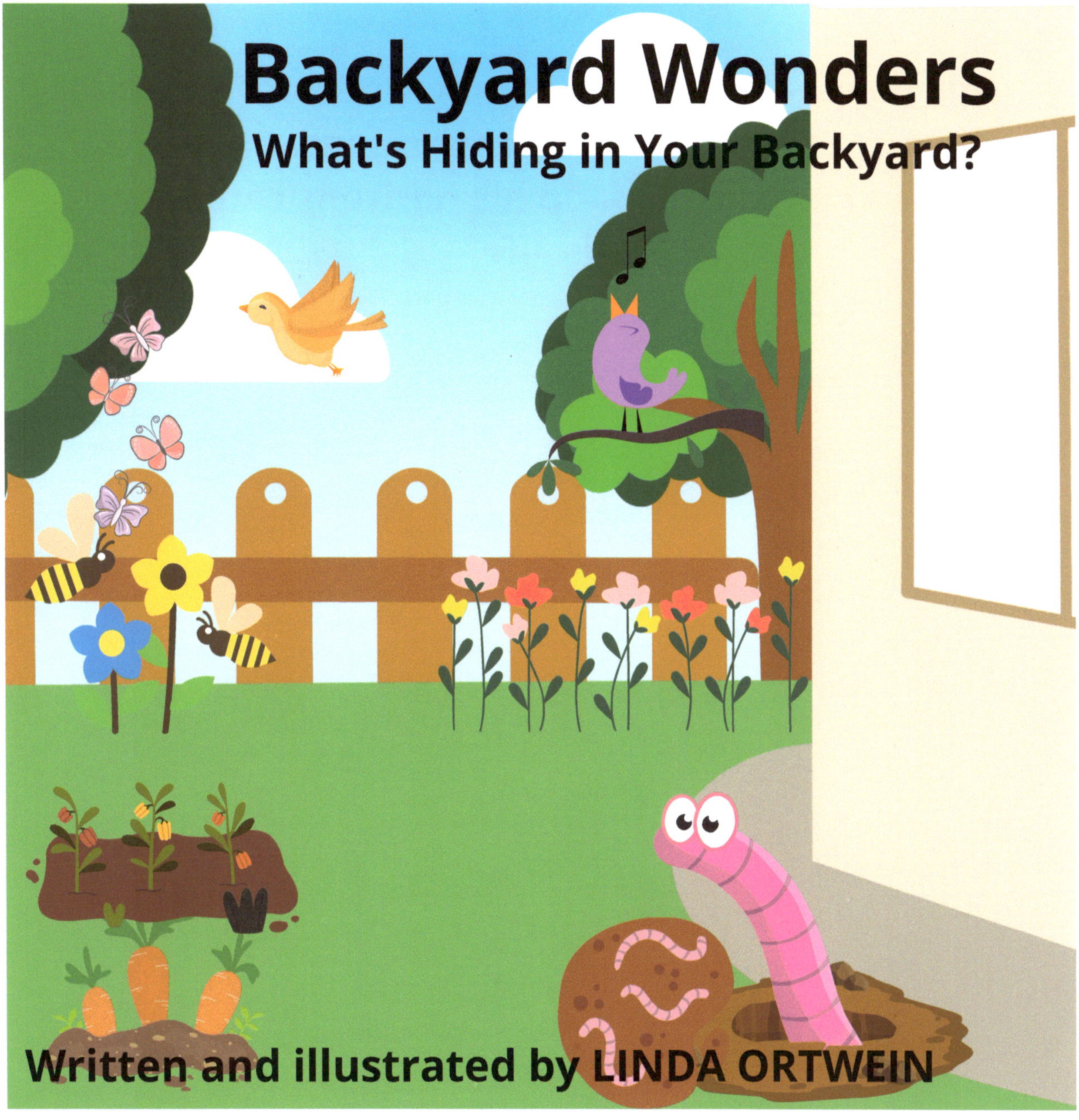

Written and illustrated by LINDA ORTWEIN

This book is dedicated to our grandson, Jameson, who has a natural curiosity for things around him. May his curiosity expand his horizons throughout his life.

Everyday before the break of dawn,

I go outside to water the lawn.

I start in the frontyard and end up in back.

I water each plant and always keep track.

And when I am done, and finished my chore,
It's time now to wander and start to explore.

What wonders are hiding in my yard and next door

My friends are the flowers,
the birds, and the bees

I study the roses and the big apple trees.

I see bugs munching grass, or just
munching on leaves

And butterflies landing on flowers in trees.

I look closely at colors and designs on their wings,

When behind me I hear
a robin who sings.

In some trees now are hidden new hummingbird nests,
A home built by the mother, she sure did her best.

Then I stand up and peak over a hedge

And in the yard next door, a red hawk lands on a ledge

Next , I move to the garden

Where new veggies now grow,
The blossoms are changing with
veggies starting to show

Then a dragonfly lands on my hand
and I freeze

But he quickly flies off, on the very next breeze.

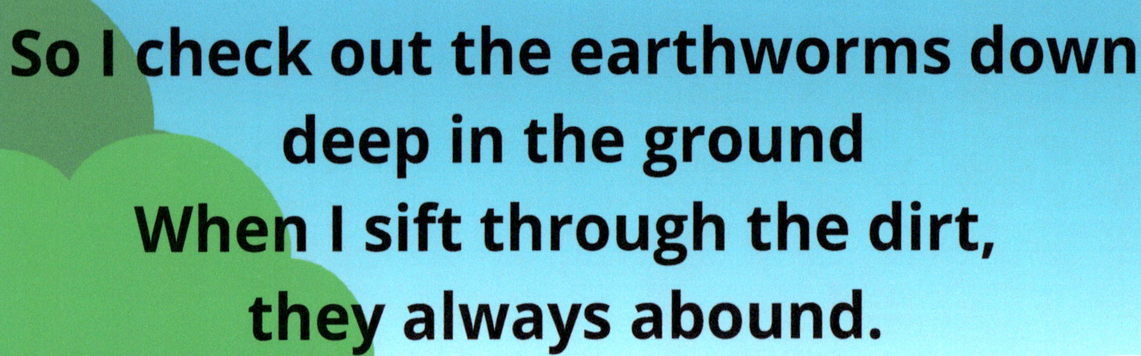

So I check out the earthworms down
deep in the ground
When I sift through the dirt,
they always abound.

When exploring is done and so is my chore,
I head back to my house and open the door.

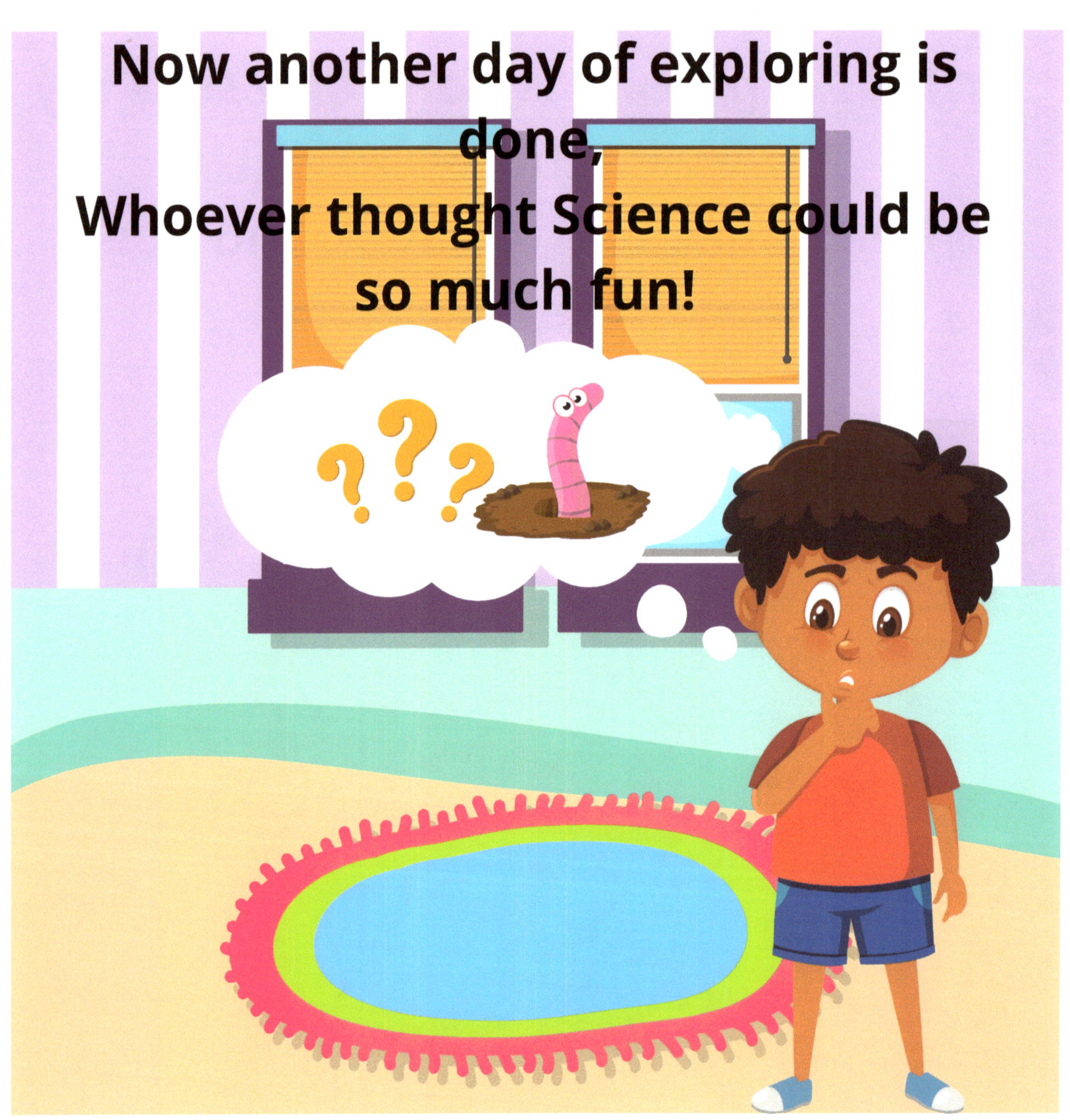

Now another day of exploring is done,
Whoever thought Science could be so much fun!